NATURE
OBSERVER

A Guided Journal

MAGGIE ENTERRIOS

Timber Press
Portland, Oregon

This journal was created with the idea of helping you experience nature in new and meaningful ways—in every season.

Maggie Enterrios's dynamic art will inspire and delight as you note important dates on the monthly calendars, chart your daily successes and goals on the trackers, and jot down to-do items on the weekly lists. These productivity features are interwoven with dozens of guided journaling prompts to help you plan your year of exploration and find intensely personal connections with nature.

At year's end, you'll have a keepsake of your favorite adventures and places.

JANUARY

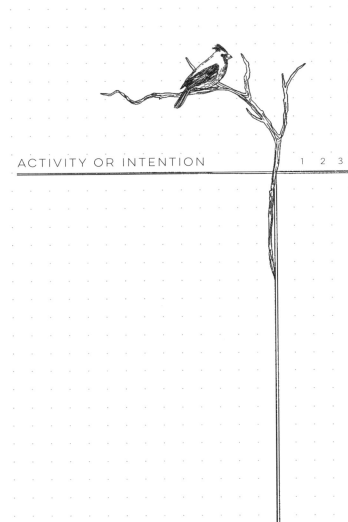

ACTIVITY OR INTENTION   1   2   3   4   5   6   7   8   9   10   11   12   13   14

JANUARY
TRACKER

15 16 17 18 19 20 21 22 23 24 25 26 27 28 29 30 31

MONDAY

TUESDAY

WEDNESDAY

THURSDAY

FRIDAY

WEEKEND

RESOLUTIONS

For living a more natural
life this year

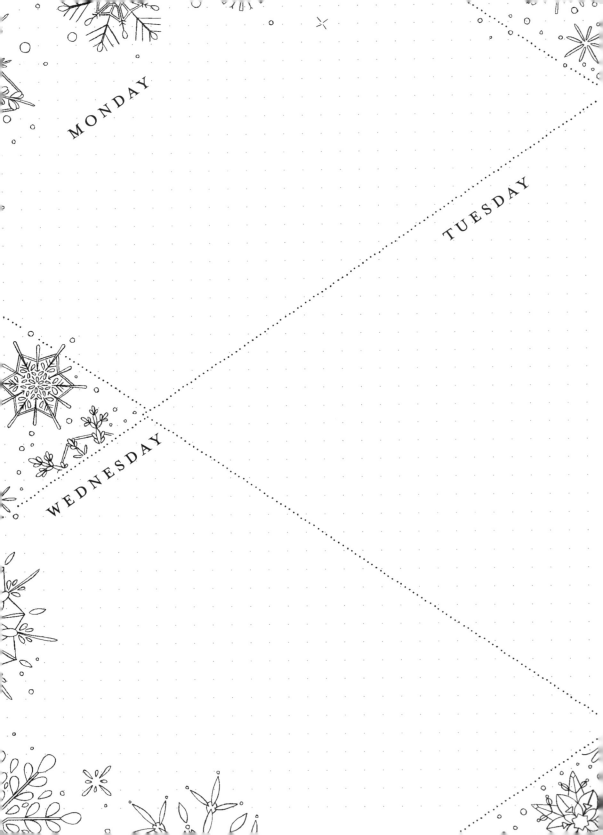

MONDAY

TUESDAY

WEDNESDAY

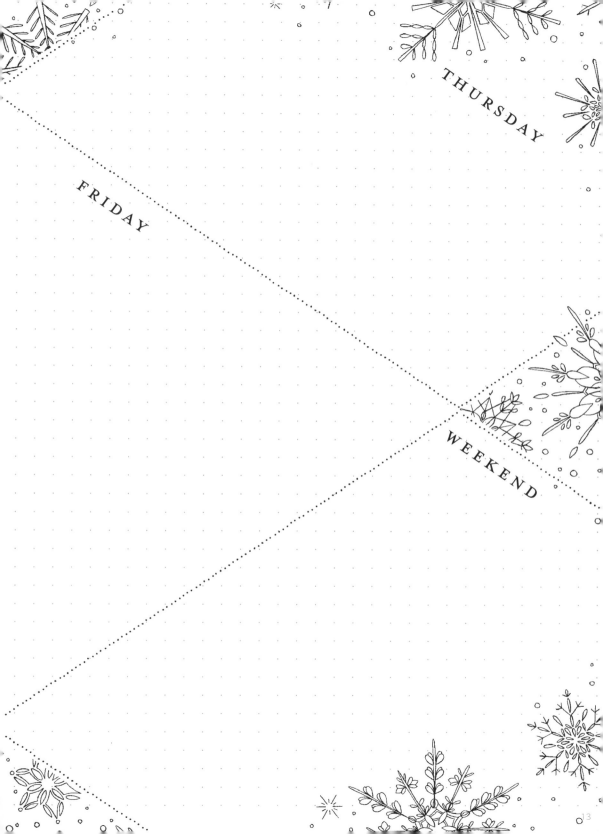

THURSDAY

FRIDAY

WEEKEND

13

Nature provides rich patterns and textures, even in the depths of winter. Look for interesting tree bark, exposed rocks, or different snowflake shapes and describe or sketch them here.

MONDAY

TUESDAY

WEDNESDAY

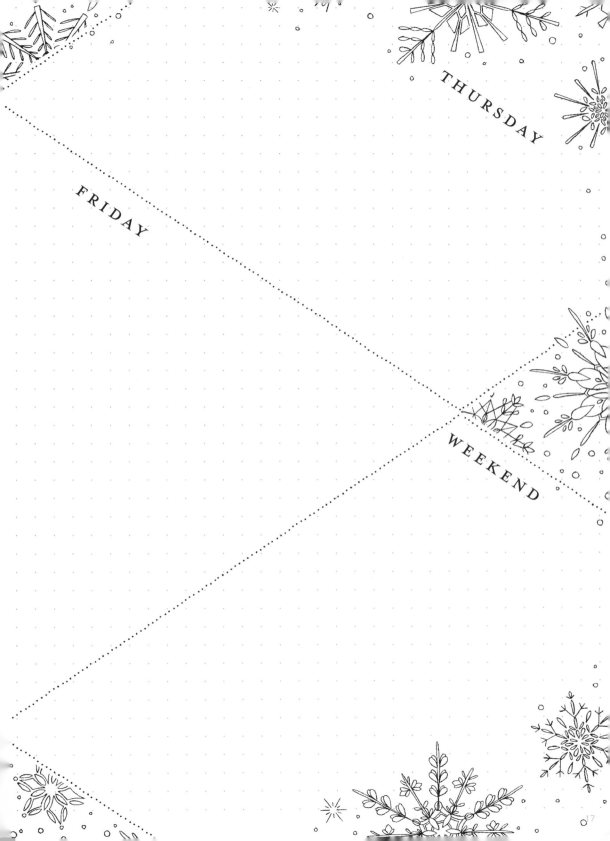

THURSDAY

FRIDAY

WEEKEND

WINTER

Walks to take:

MONDAY

TUESDAY

WEDNESDAY

THURSDAY

FRIDAY

WEEKEND

Changes in my neighborhood that only
happen during winter:

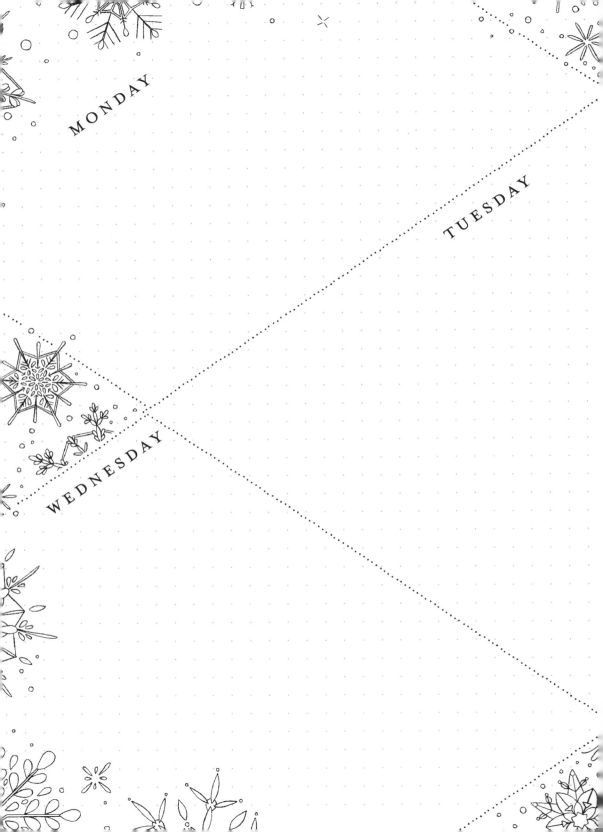

MONDAY

TUESDAY

WEDNESDAY

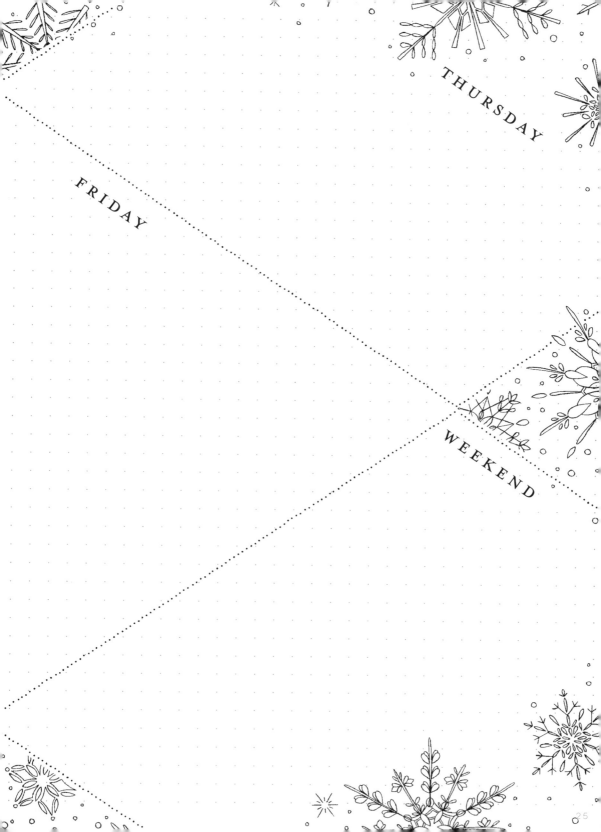

THURSDAY

FRIDAY

WEEKEND

FEBRUARY

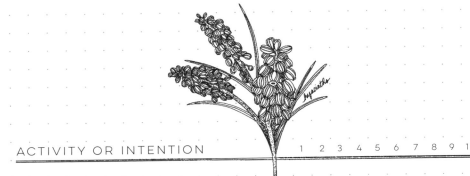

ACTIVITY OR INTENTION   1 2 3 4 5 6 7 8 9 10 11 12 13 14

FEBRUARY

TRACKER

15 16 17 18 19 20 21 22 23 24 25 26 27 28 29

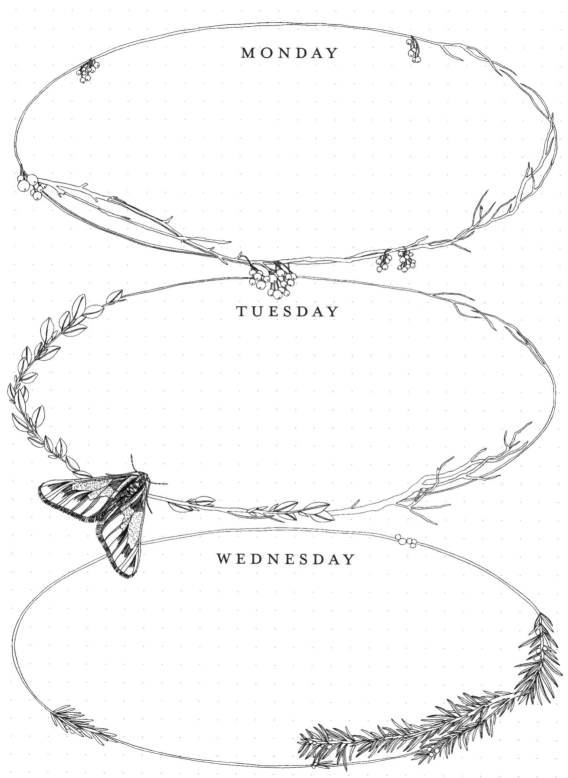

MONDAY

TUESDAY

WEDNESDAY

THURSDAY

FRIDAY

WEEKEND

Take a cold-weather hike to a place where less vegetation lays bare amazing geological formations. Sketch the route for the hike here.

Draw or describe ten things you see during your hike.

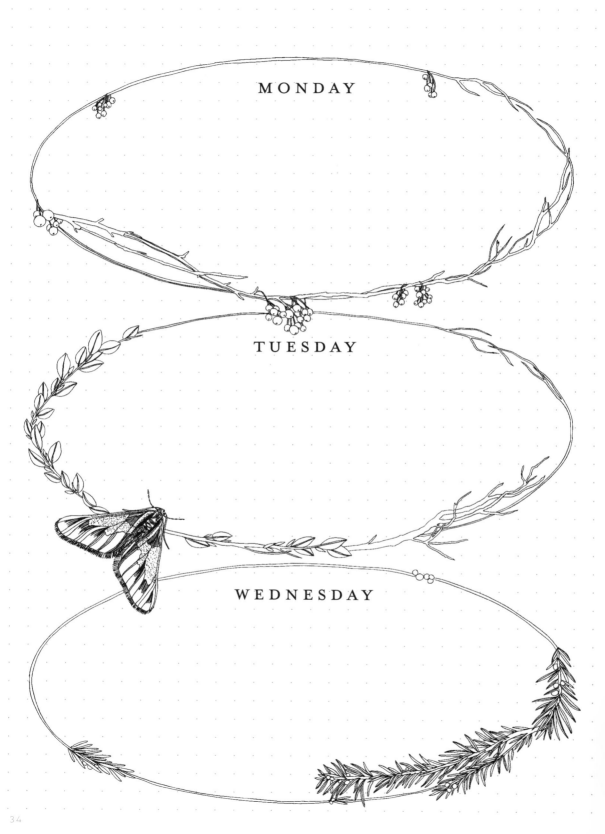

MONDAY

TUESDAY

WEDNESDAY

THURSDAY

FRIDAY

WEEKEND

Visit a river, lake, or stream near you that you plan to return to in each season. Take note of how the water looks, how high it is, or how it is moving each time you visit.

MONDAY

TUESDAY

WEDNESDAY

THURSDAY

FRIDAY

WEEKEND

My favorite type of winter weather is:

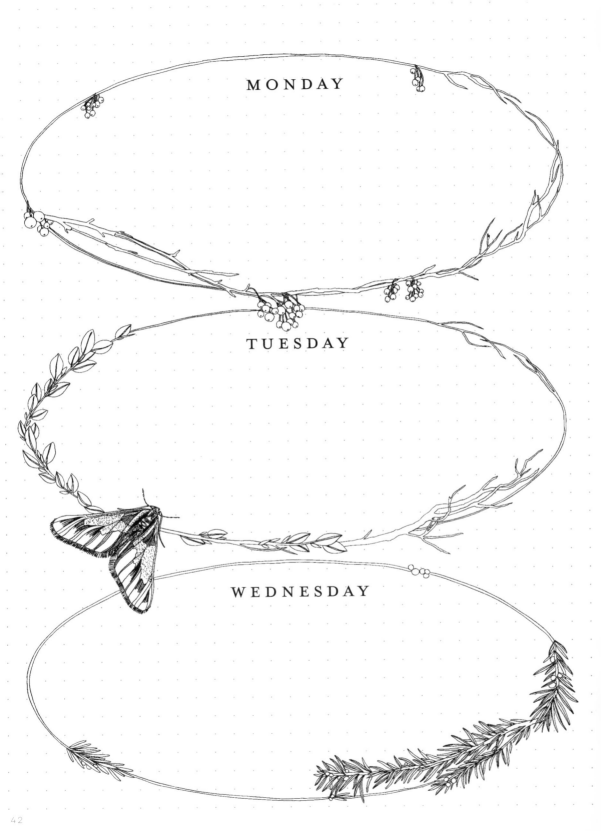

MONDAY

TUESDAY

WEDNESDAY

THURSDAY

FRIDAY

WEEKEND

Look for one surprising thing in nature every day for a week. Describe or sketch it, and note where you saw it.

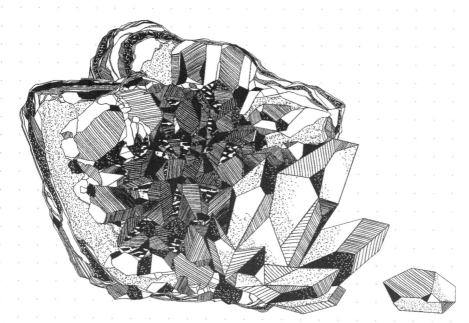

MONDAY

TUESDAY

WEDNESDAY

THURSDAY

FRIDAY

WEEKEND

MARCH

ACTIVITY OR INTENTION   1 2 3 4 5 6 7 8 9 10 11 12 13 14

MARCH

TRACKER

15 16 17 18 19 20 21 22 23 24 25 26 27 28 29 30 31

MONDAY

TUESDAY

WEDNESDAY

THURSDAY

FRIDAY

WEEKEND

Ask three friends for their three favorite hikes,
bike routes or outdoor desinations in your region.

Friend

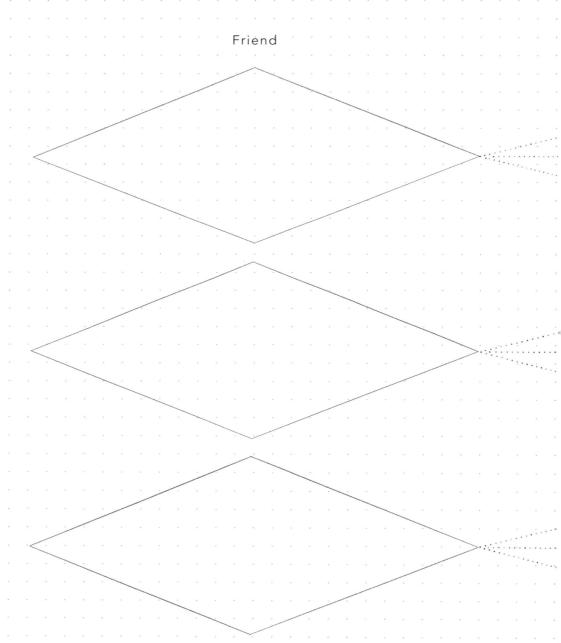

Suggestions

MONDAY

TUESDAY

WEDNESDAY

THURSDAY

FRIDAY

WEEKEND

Winter birds I have seen, and where:

Birds with migratory paths near me I might be able to see later in the season:

MONDAY

TUESDAY

WEDNESDAY

THURSDAY

FRIDAY

WEEKEND

The days are lengthening. Keep track of sunrise and sunset times for two weeks to remind yourself of this, and jot down a note about the quality of light or the weather each day.

MONDAY

TUESDAY

WEDNESDAY

THURSDAY

FRIDAY

WEEKEND

Record the dates of when trees in your neighborhood begin to bloom:

Apple
Blossoms

MONDAY

TUESDAY

WEDNESDAY

THURSDAY

FRIDAY

WEEKEND

APRIL

ACTIVITY OR INTENTION   1   2   3   4   5   6   7   8   9   10   11   12   13   14

APRIL

TRACKER

15 16 17 18 19 20 21 22 23 24 25 26 27 28 29 30

MONDAY

TUESDAY

WEDNESDAY

THURSDAY

FRIDAY

WEEKEND

Sketch or describe April-blooming flowers
or wildflowers you see around you.

BISHOP'S HAT

daffodil

HYACINTH

Leopard's
Bane

MONDAY

TUESDAY

WEDNESDAY

THURSDAY

FRIDAY

WEEKEND

PACKING LIST

Things I should always remember to bring in my
hiking backpack:

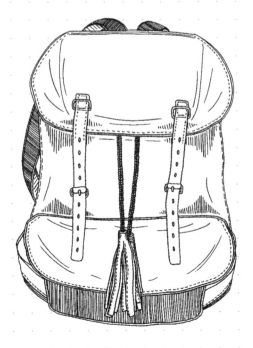

MONDAY

TUESDAY

WEDNESDAY

THURSDAY

FRIDAY

WEEKEND

CAMPING EQUIPMENT

Wish List

MONDAY

TUESDAY

WEDNESDAY

THURSDAY

FRIDAY

WEEKEND

Describe or sketch at least ten things you see
under your feet that are harbingers of spring.

MONDAY

TUESDAY

WEDNESDAY

THURSDAY

FRIDAY

WEEKEND

MAY

ACTIVITY OR INTENTION   1   2   3   4   5   6   7   8   9   10   11   12   13   14

California poppies

MAY

TRACKER

15 16 17 18 19 20 21 22 23 24 25 26 27 28 29 30 31

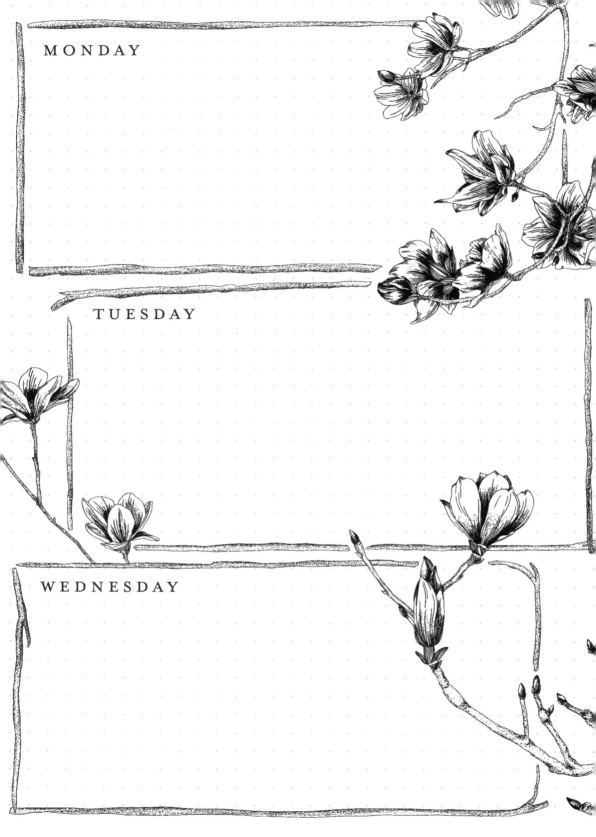

MONDAY

TUESDAY

WEDNESDAY

THURSDAY

FRIDAY

WEEKEND

The leaves are back! Take a walk and look for as
many of the leaf shapes as you can find from the
facing page. List the names of the trees they
belong to here:

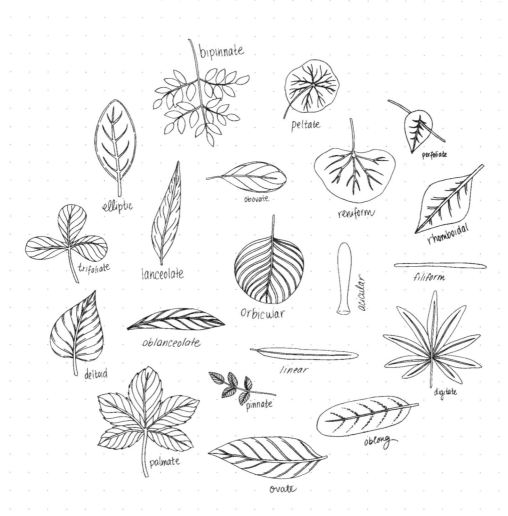

bipinnate

peltate

perfoliate

elliptic

obovate

reniform

rhomboidal

trifoliate

lanceolate

orbicular

acicular

filiform

deltoid

oblanceolate

linear

digitate

palmate

pinnate

oblong

ovate

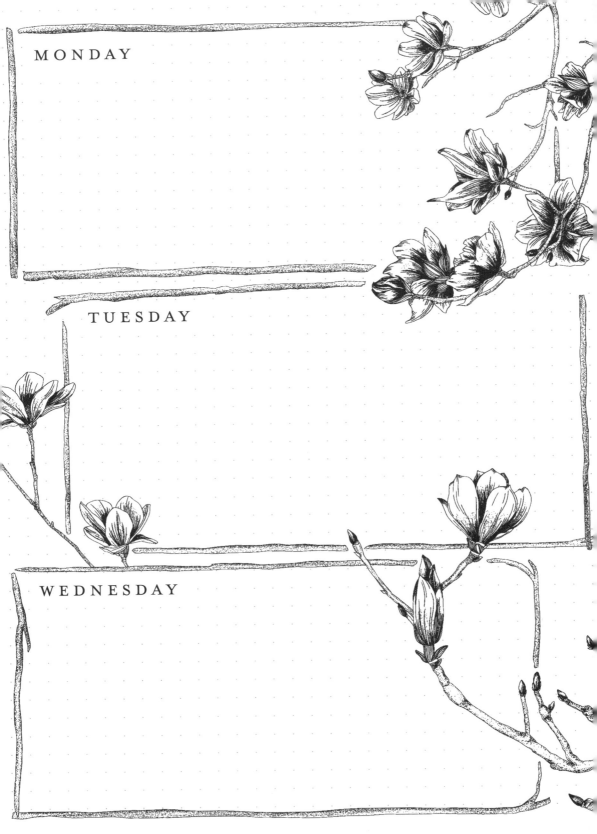

MONDAY

TUESDAY

WEDNESDAY

THURSDAY

FRIDAY

WEEKEND

Celebrate things being back in bloom by finding
wildflowers in your neighborhood or nearby
nature preserve with three petals, four petals,
and five petals—or many. Identify and sketch
or describe them.

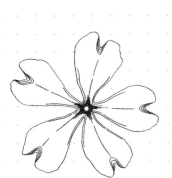

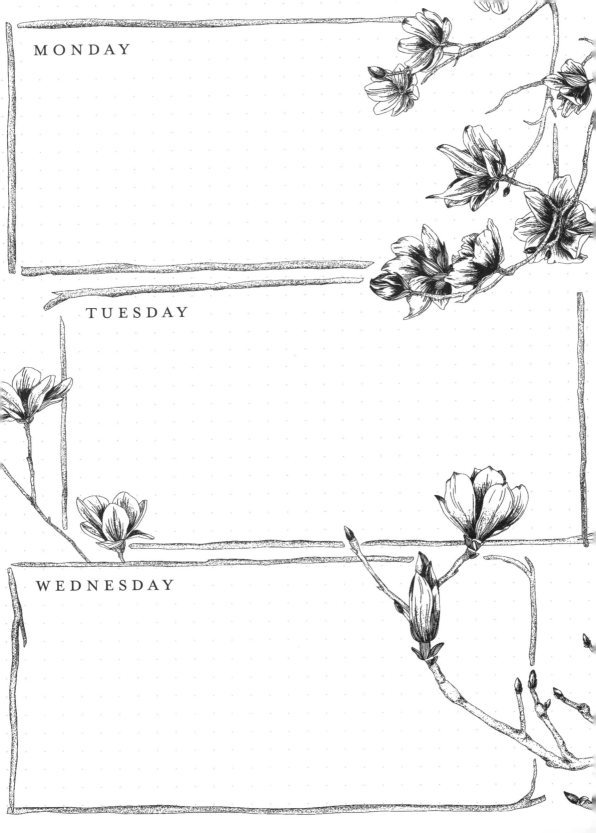

MONDAY

TUESDAY

WEDNESDAY

THURSDAY

FRIDAY

WEEKEND

Make your next walk a scavenger hunt by looking
for something natural in every color.

red

orange

yellow

green

blue

violet

brown

black

gray

white

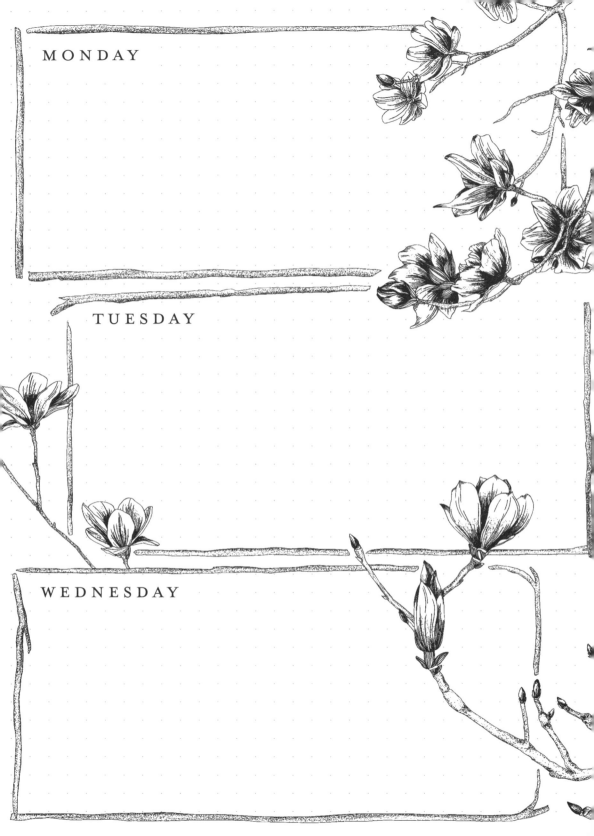

MONDAY

TUESDAY

WEDNESDAY

THURSDAY

FRIDAY

WEEKEND

Sketch or describe the progress of something
growing near your home by tracking it every day
for two weeks, such as a vining plant up a trellis,
the density of a tree's canopy, or the number of
flower buds in a pot.

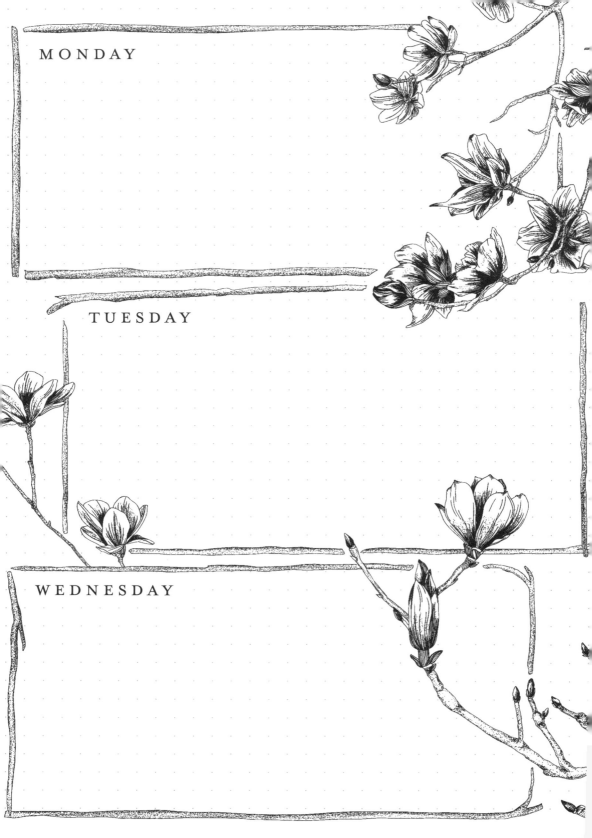

MONDAY

TUESDAY

WEDNESDAY

THURSDAY

FRIDAY

WEEKEND

JUNE

ACTIVITY OR INTENTION   1   2   3   4   5   6   7   8   9   10 11 12 13 14

JUNE

TRACKER

15 16 17 18 19 20 21 22 23 24 25 26 27 28 29 30

MONDAY

TUESDAY

WEDNESDAY

THURSDAY

FRIDAY

WEEKEND

Sit in a favorite park or nature preserve and sketch or describe what you see, hear, smell, and feel around you in a fifteen-minute window.

MONDAY

TUESDAY

WEDNESDAY

THURSDAY

FRIDAY

WEEKEND

Top outdoor destinations to visit this summer:

Mountain:

Lake:

Beach:

River:

Canyon:

Valley:

MONDAY

TUESDAY

WEDNESDAY

THURSDAY

FRIDAY

WEEKEND

Recipes to try with fresh local produce or with
edible items that I've foraged during my excursions:

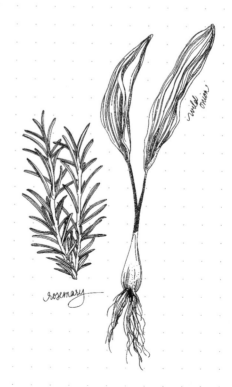

rosemary

wild onion

MONDAY

TUESDAY

WEDNESDAY

THURSDAY

FRIDAY

WEEKEND

On the solstice, make plans for how to use those extra hours of summer daylight:

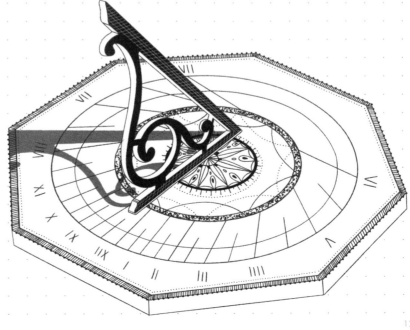

MONDAY

TUESDAY

WEDNESDAY

THURSDAY

FRIDAY

WEEKEND

JULY

ACTIVITY OR INTENTION   1   2   3   4   5   6   7   8   9   10 11 12 13 14

J U L Y

T R A C K E R

15 16 17 18 19 20 21 22 23 24 25 26 27 28 29 30 31

MONDAY

TUESDAY

WEDNESDAY

THURSDAY

FRIDAY

WEEKEND

List or sketch the wildlife you have seen this
year—butterflies, bees, birds, caterpillars, moths,
even deer or larger mammals. Note the time of
day you saw it and where.

COTTONWOOD leaf BEETLE

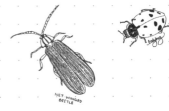

NET-WINGED BEETLE

MONDAY

TUESDAY

WEDNESDAY

THURSDAY

FRIDAY

WEEKEND

FAVORITE QUOTES

about summertime:

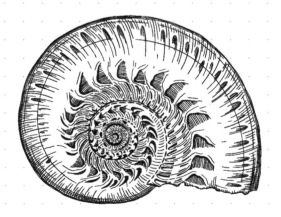

MONDAY

TUESDAY

WEDNESDAY

THURSDAY

FRIDAY

WEEKEND

Sketch or describe the way the sky looks and sounds and how the air feels just before, during, and after a big summer thunderstorm.

MONDAY

TUESDAY

WEDNESDAY

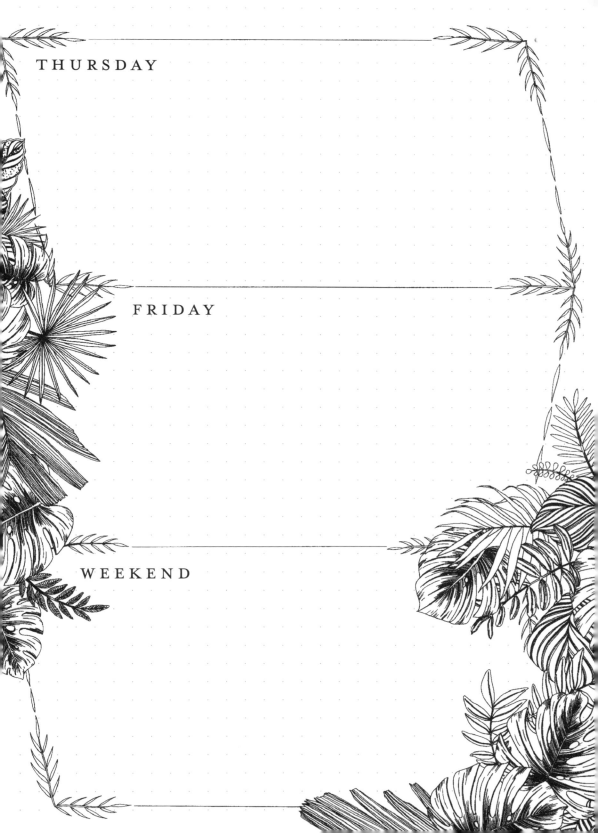

THURSDAY

FRIDAY

WEEKEND

Turn over a fallen log or stump on your next walk.
Sketch or describe what you see growing and
living on or underneath it.

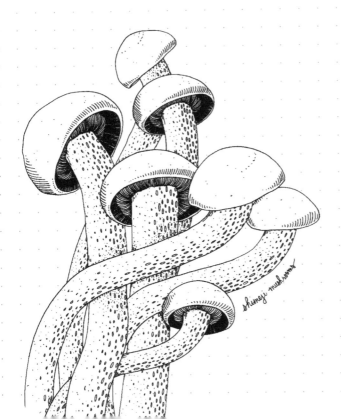

shimeji mushrooms

MONDAY

TUESDAY

WEDNESDAY

THURSDAY

FRIDAY

WEEKEND

AUGUST

ACTIVITY OR INTENTION   1 2 3 4 5 6 7 8 9 10 11 12 13 14

AUGUST
TRACKER

15 16 17 18 19 20 21 22 23 24 25 26 27 28 29 30 31

MONDAY

TUESDAY

WEDNESDAY

THURSDAY

FRIDAY

WEEKEND

SUMMER EXCURSIONS

Place

Weather

Memories

MONDAY

TUESDAY

WEDNESDAY

THURSDAY

FRIDAY

WEEKEND

NATIONAL PARK

Bucket List

MONDAY

TUESDAY

WEDNESDAY

THURSDAY

FRIDAY

WEEKEND

Observations of the sky during a summer meteor shower:

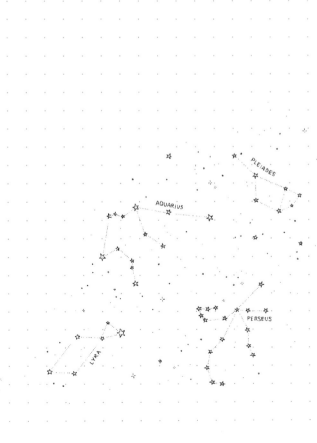

MONDAY

TUESDAY

WEDNESDAY

THURSDAY

FRIDAY

WEEKEND

Describe or sketch ten things you found on
a beach or lakeshore.

MONDAY

TUESDAY

WEDNESDAY

THURSDAY

FRIDAY

WEEKEND

SEPTEMBER

ACTIVITY OR INTENTION   1   2   3   4   5   6   7   8   9   10   11   12   13   14

SEPTEMBER

TRACKER

15 16 17 18 19 20 21 22 23 24 25 26 27 28 29 30

MONDAY

TUESDAY

WEDNESDAY

THURSDAY

FRIDAY

WEEKEND

Visit a favorite body of water for the last time this warm season. Sketch or describe what you notice about its volume, inhabitants, or temperature.

MONDAY

TUESDAY

WEDNESDAY

THURSDAY

FRIDAY

WEEKEND

OBSERVATIONS

Stop to observe nature for ten minutes every day
for a week as the season eases into fall.

Date   Time   Weather

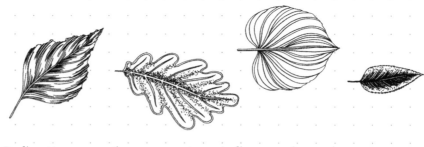

Reflections on the way nature influenced my day:

MONDAY

TUESDAY

WEDNESDAY

THURSDAY

FRIDAY

WEEKEND

MIGRATING BIRD TRACKER

Date   Species

Number observed and observations:

MONDAY

TUESDAY

WEDNESDAY

THURSDAY

FRIDAY

WEEKEND

Ways I see small creatures around me preparing for winter:

MONDAY

TUESDAY

WEDNESDAY

THURSDAY

FRIDAY

WEEKEND

OCTOBER

ACTIVITY OR INTENTION   1 2 3 4 5 6 7 8 9 10 11 12 13 14

OCTOBER

TRACKER

15 16 17 18 19 20 21 22 23 24 25 26 27 28 29 30 31

MONDAY

TUESDAY

WEDNESDAY

THURSDAY

FRIDAY

WEEKEND

As the days begin to shorten, observe your own yard or a favorite outdoor space at both seven o'clock in the morning and seven o'clock at night, noting the differences you see.

MONDAY

TUESDAY

WEDNESDAY

THURSDAY

FRIDAY

WEEKEND

Jot down words or phrases you associate with
fall, and record any sensory memories they bring
to mind.

sweetgum

milkweed

MONDAY

TUESDAY

WEDNESDAY

THURSDAY

FRIDAY

WEEKEND

Outline the shapes of a few fallen leaves here, or make a rubbing and paste it in.

MONDAY

TUESDAY

WEDNESDAY

THURSDAY

FRIDAY

WEEKEND

Sketch or describe spiders you see, their webs, and note where you found them.

MONDAY

TUESDAY

WEDNESDAY

THURSDAY

FRIDAY

WEEKEND

NOVEMBER

WITCH
HAZEL

ACTIVITY OR INTENTION   1   2   3   4   5   6   7   8   9   10   11   12   13   14

NOVEMBER

TRACKER

15 16 17 18 19 20 21 22 23 24 25 26 27 28 29 30

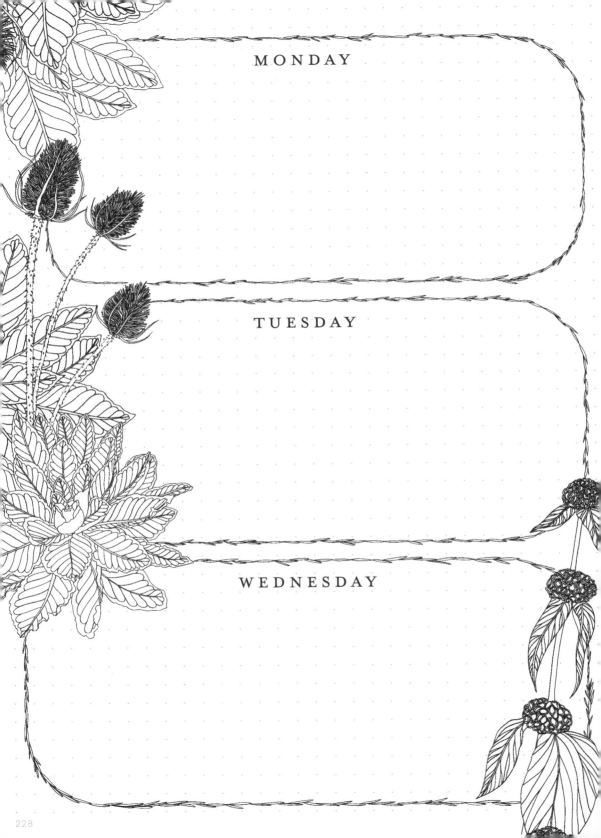

MONDAY

TUESDAY

WEDNESDAY

THURSDAY

FRIDAY

WEEKEND

There are many shades of "brown." Look around you for materials in as many varieties of the color as you can. Sketch or describe them here.

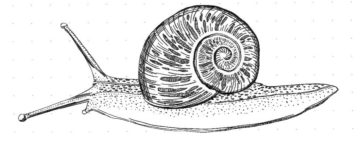

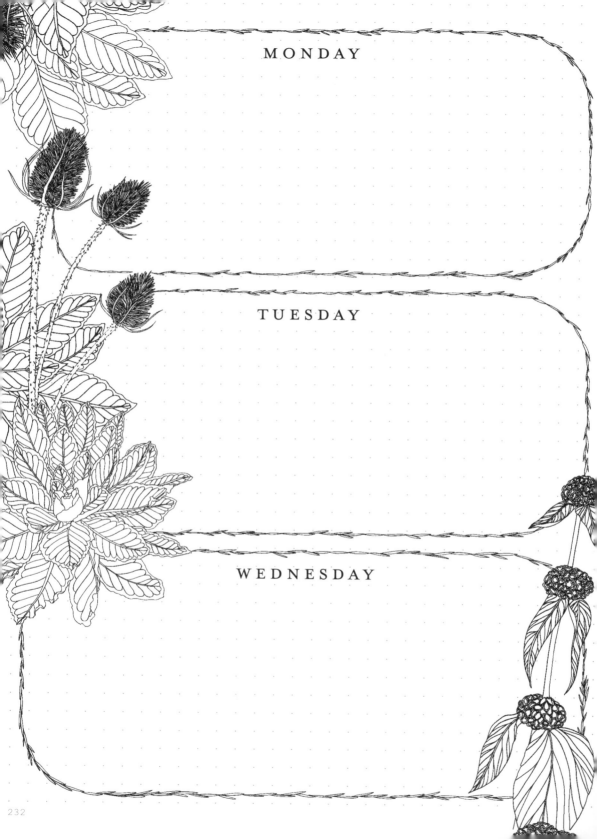

MONDAY

TUESDAY

WEDNESDAY

THURSDAY

FRIDAY

WEEKEND

OBSERVATIONS

The first ice of the season:

Date   Location   Appearance

Comments:

MONDAY

TUESDAY

WEDNESDAY

THURSDAY

FRIDAY

WEEKEND

Draw or describe how your favorite deciduous
tree looks now that the leaves are down.

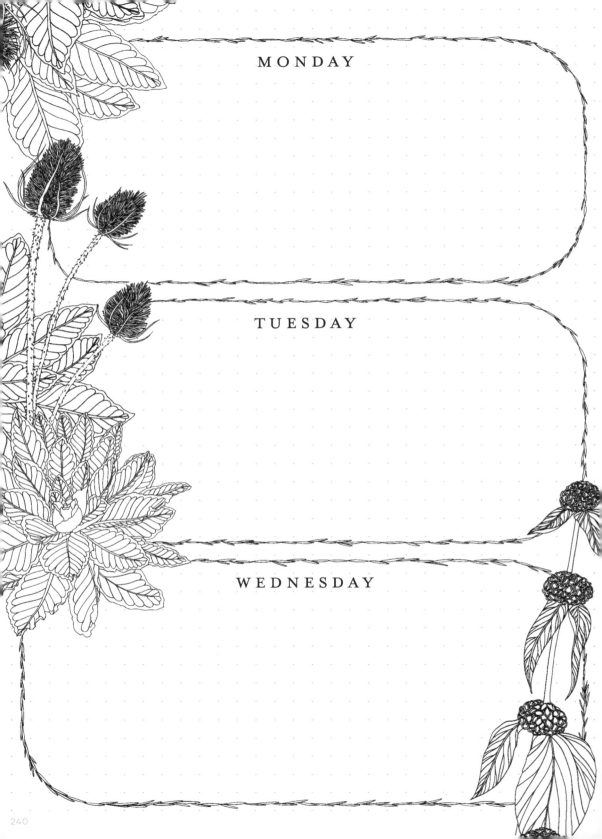

MONDAY

TUESDAY

WEDNESDAY

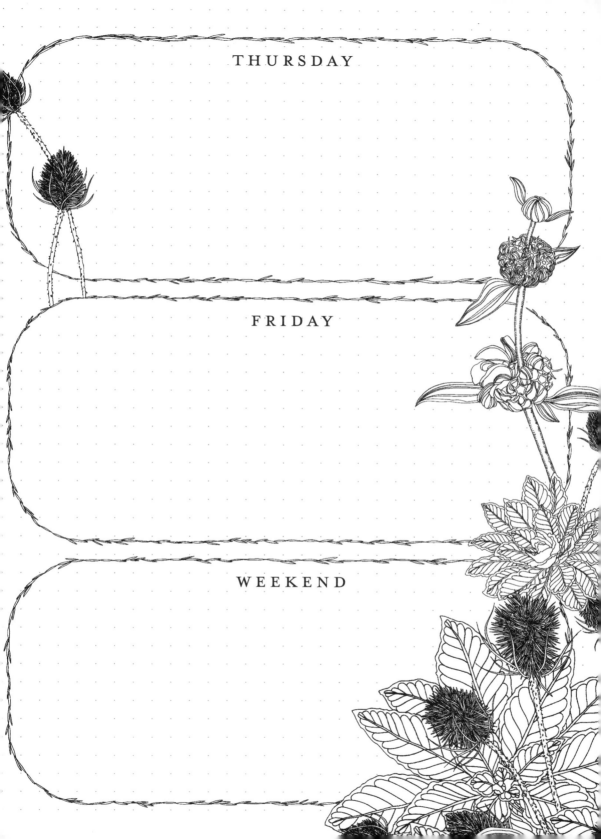

THURSDAY

FRIDAY

WEEKEND

Autumn harvests yield many delicious fruits and
vegetables. List the flavors you are most looking
forward to:

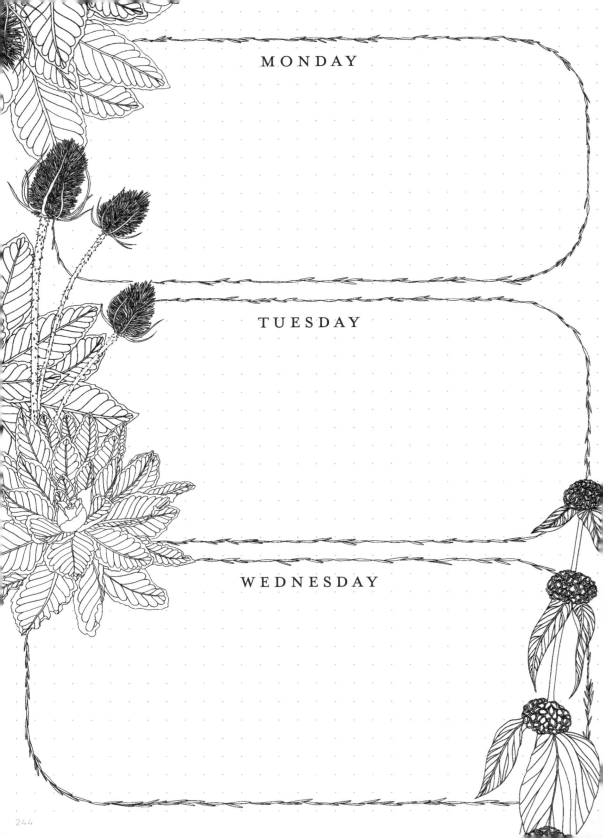

MONDAY

TUESDAY

WEDNESDAY

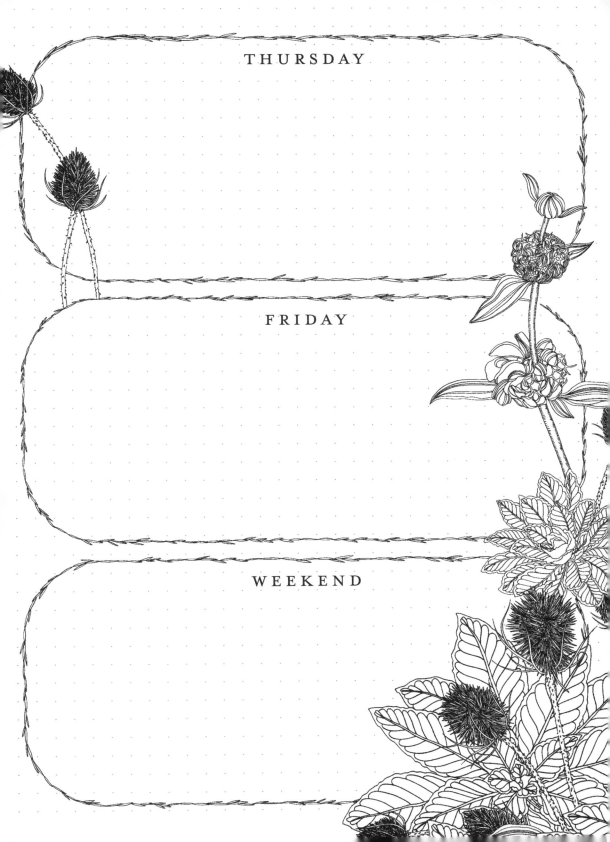

THURSDAY

FRIDAY

WEEKEND

DECEMBER

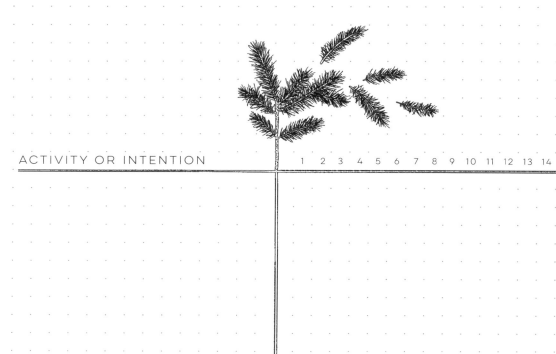

ACTIVITY OR INTENTION   1   2   3   4   5   6   7   8   9   10   11   12   13   14

DECEMBER

TRACKER

15 16 17 18 19 20 21 22 23 24 25 26 27 28 29 30 31

MONDAY

TUESDAY

WEDNESDAY

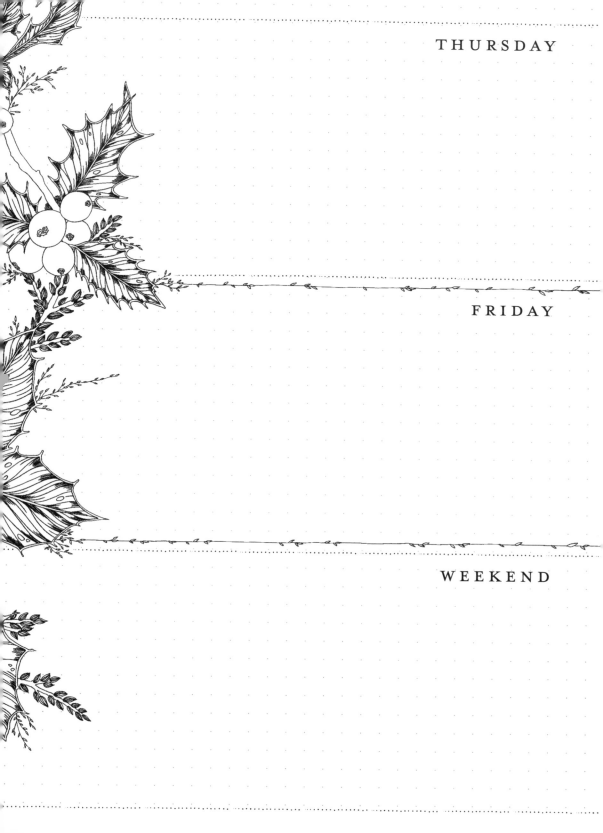

THURSDAY

FRIDAY

WEEKEND

Things I see in the winter landscape as viewed
through my window:

MONDAY

TUESDAY

WEDNESDAY

THURSDAY

FRIDAY

WEEKEND

Draw or describe evergreen trees and shrubs
that are still providing greenery in the winter
landscape.

MONDAY

TUESDAY

WEDNESDAY

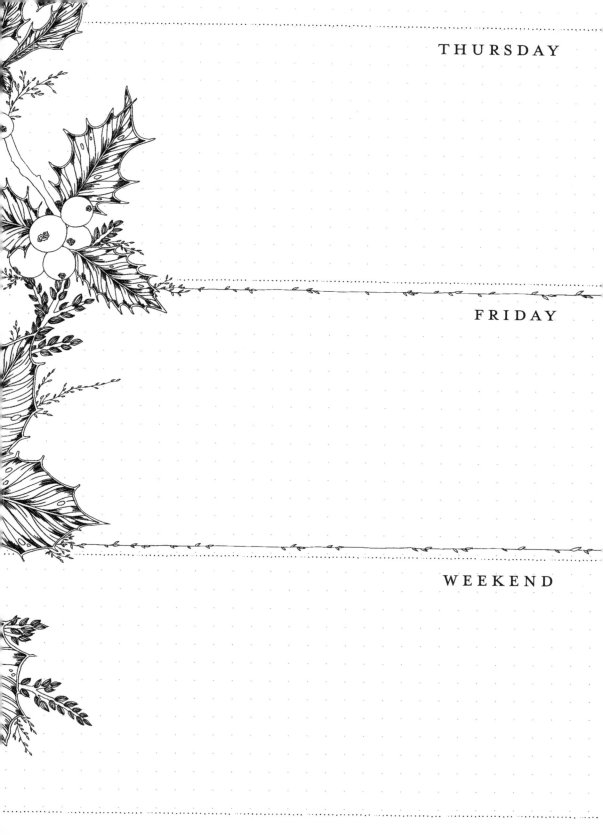

THURSDAY

FRIDAY

WEEKEND

Look for, sketch, and try to identify signs of
animal life around you. Do you see burrowed
holes or tracks in snow?

MONDAY

TUESDAY

WEDNESDAY

THURSDAY

FRIDAY

WEEKEND

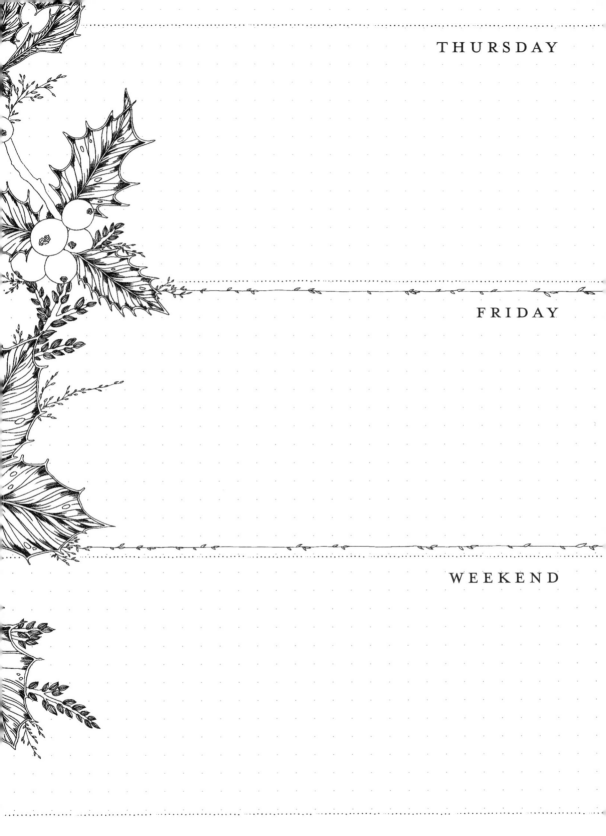

My favorite memories of being outdoors this year:

favorite memories

MONDAY

TUESDAY

WEDNESDAY

THURSDAY

FRIDAY

WEEKEND

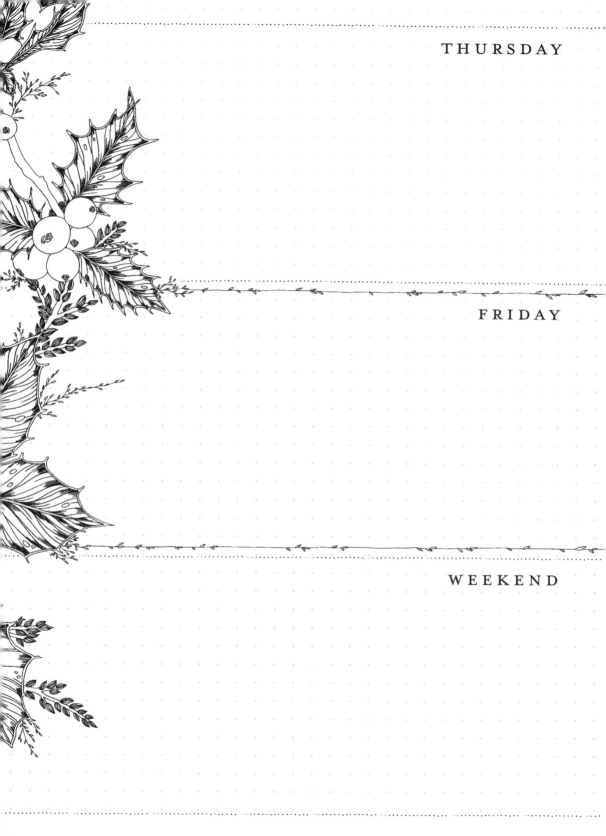

Field notes:

Field notes: